DINOSAUR SCIENCE

WHO ATE THE DINOSAURS?

BY DR. DAVE HONE
AND DAVE SMITH

Enslow PUBLISHING

Published in 2026 by Enslow Publishing, LLC
2544 Clinton Street
Buffalo, NY 14224

First published in Great Britain in 2023 by Wayland

Editors: Christina Webb and Elise Short
Design: Emma DeBanks

Printed in China

CPSIA compliance information: Batch #QW26ENS: For further information contact Enslow Publishing LLC, New York, New York at 1-800-398-2504.

Please visit our website, www.enslowpublishing.com. For a free color catalog of all our high-quality books, call toll free 1-800-398-2504 or fax 1-877-980-4454.

Cataloging-in-Publication Data
Names: Hone, David (Paleontologist), author. | Smith, Dave, illustrator.
Title: Who ate the dinosaurs? / by Dr. Dave Hone, illustrated by Dave Smith.
Description: Buffalo, NY : Enslow Publishing, 2026. | Series: Dinosaur science | Includes glossary and index.
Identifiers: ISBN 9781978547285 (pbk.) | ISBN 9781978547292 (library bound) | ISBN 9781978547308 (ebook)
Subjects: LCSH: Dinosaurs--Juvenile literature. | Extinct reptiles--Juvenile literature. | Paleontology--Juvenile literature.
Classification: LCC QE862.D5 H66 2026 | DDC 567.9--dc23

Find us on

CONTENTS

A WORLD OF LIVING THINGS

Dinosaur fossils – the remains or traces of once-living things that have turned to stone over time – are found in rocks that date back to a time we call the Mesozoic Era. The Mesozoic Era lasted from about 245 to 65 million years ago.

A Long, Long Time Ago

The first dinosaurs, such as *Nyasasaurus* – the earliest known dinosaur to be discovered in modern-day Tanzania – appeared around 230 million years ago. The dinosaurs then roamed Earth for about 165 million years. This might sound like a very long time, but Earth is over a billion years old: that's a thousand million years!

Wonderful World of Living Things

The dinosaurs are the most famous group from the Mesozoic Era, but they lived alongside many other animals and plants. You could find everything from giant marine reptiles to early marsupials (these include the koalas and kangaroos of today), as well as frogs, butterflies, ferns, and monkey puzzle trees. It's hard to believe, but some of these creatures ate dinosaurs!

Cretaceous Period

EVER CHANGING!

The surface of Earth is changing all the time. Earthquakes and volcanic eruptions can change the shape of landscapes or even form new land. Huge blocks of rock are constantly moving very, very slowly, which means the continents are spreading out.

Continent Break-up

The world looked very different 250 million years ago. All of Earth's land was bunched up into one giant continent called Pangaea. It then broke up into two big chunks, then split again and drifted to form shapes that led to the familiar continents we have now.

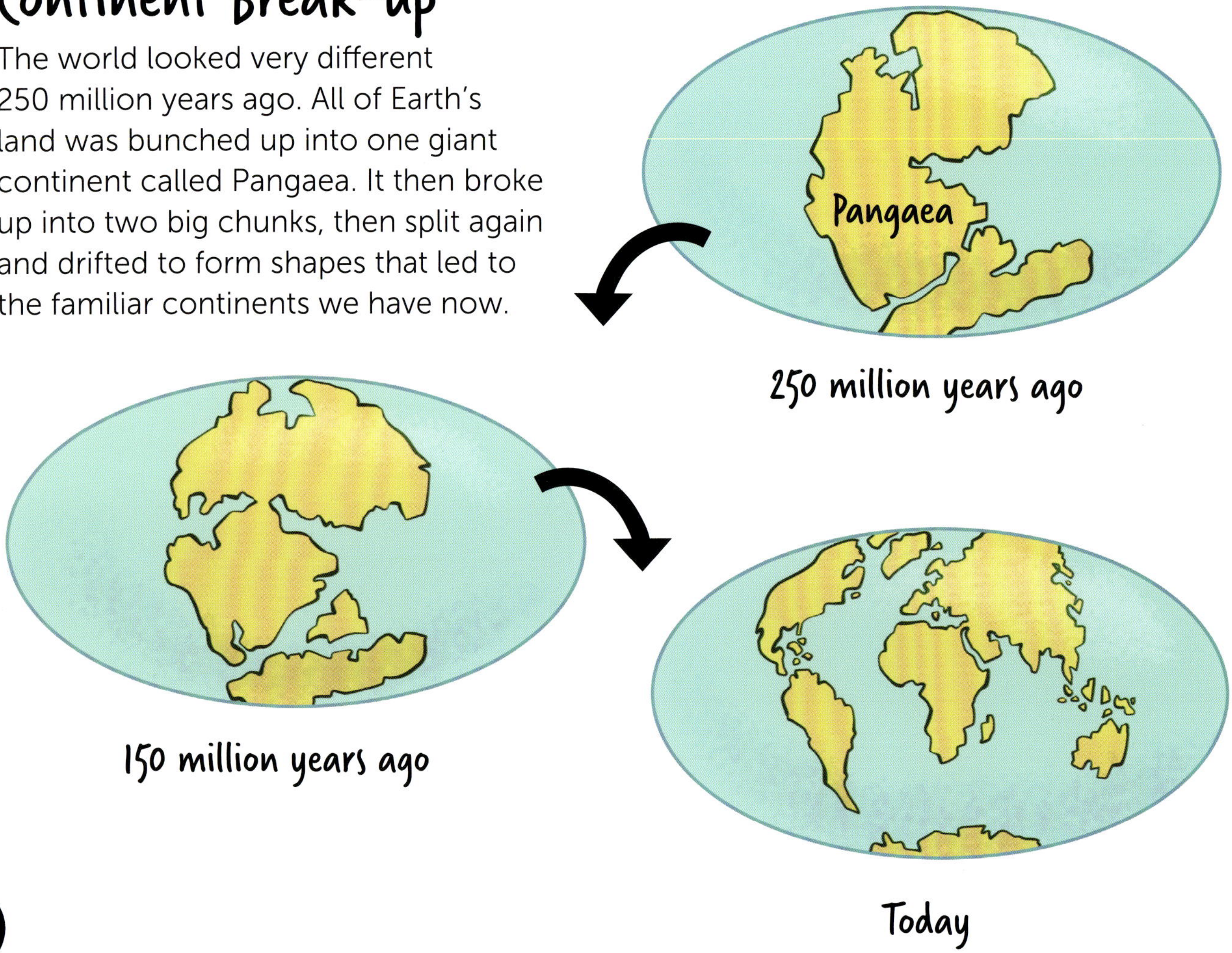

Dealing With Change

This was a time of real change for the dinosaurs and other ancient animals. Where there was once one big piece of land, oceans and seas broke it up into new parts. The climate also changed – some areas went from hot and dry to wet. This all had an effect on these creatures, who changed over time to suit and survive where they lived.

EVERYWHERE AT ONCE

In books and films, dinosaurs are often shown to be living in swamps and rainforests, but they actually lived all over the world in every type of environment you can think of.

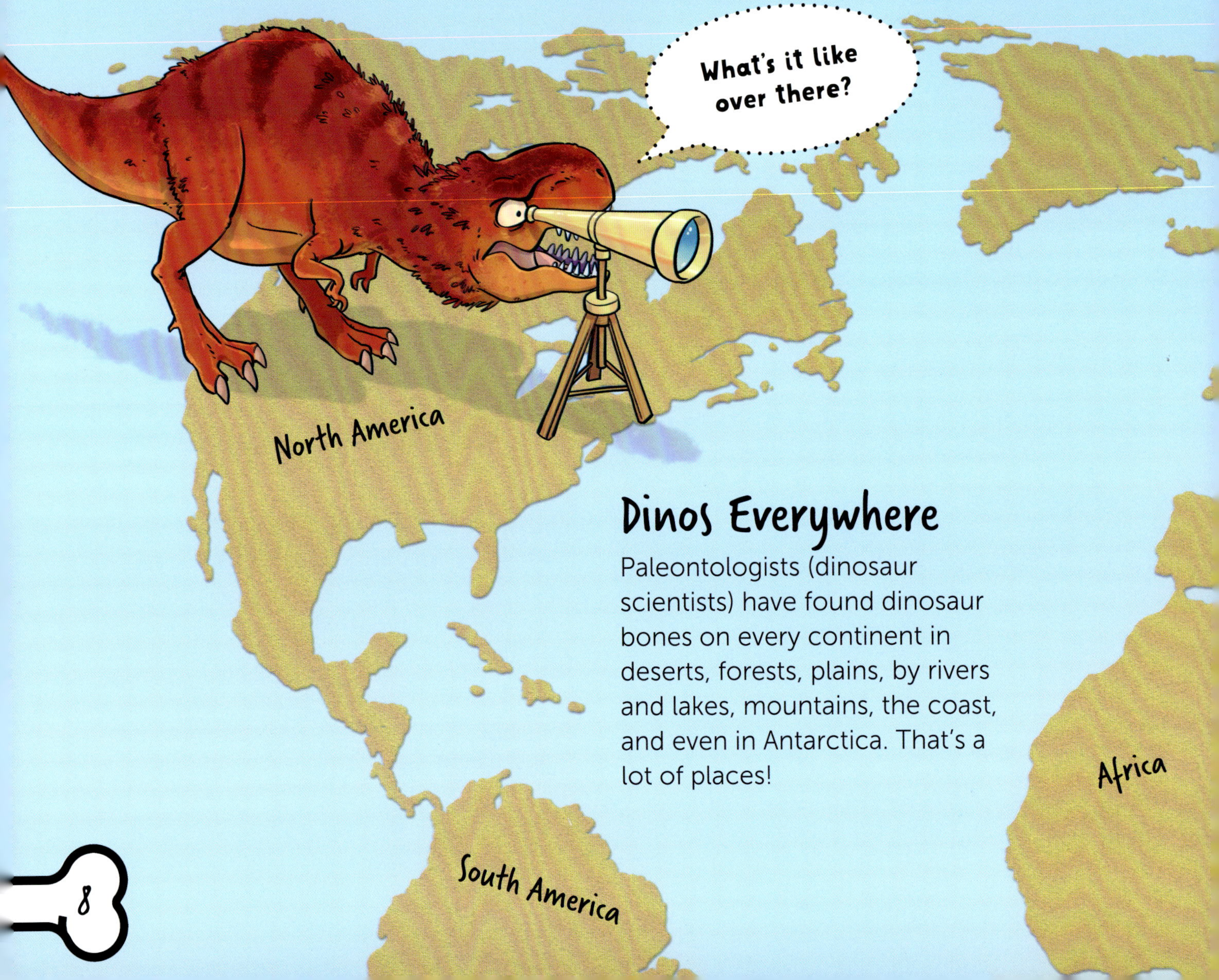

Dinos Everywhere

Paleontologists (dinosaur scientists) have found dinosaur bones on every continent in deserts, forests, plains, by rivers and lakes, mountains, the coast, and even in Antarctica. That's a lot of places!

All Over the World

Different types of dinosaur existed in different times and places. *Tyrannosaurus* and *Stegosaurus* both lived in what is now North America, but about 80 million years apart. *Tyrannosaurus* lived at a similar time to *Velociraptor*, but they never met because *Velociraptor* lived in Asia.

DID YOU KNOW?

Scientists have now found dinosaurs in over 150 different countries across the globe!

PLANT LIFE

Lots of different plants grew during the Mesozoic Era (see page 5), and many examples of them still exist today.

Ferns Then Pines

Early on, ferns dominated. There were huge forests of tree ferns. Later, they became less common, as conifers and pines – such as spiky monkey puzzle trees – took over.

Hello, Flowers!

The Jurassic Period was between 200 and 145 million years ago and toward the end of it, the first flowering plants appeared. The first flowers belonged to small water plants, which would later evolve to grow on land and produce everything from grasses to giant trees. Early flowers used the wind to move pollen between flowers, but later ones attracted insects to do the job.

DID YOU KNOW?

Grasses were rare in dinosaur times and only appeared toward the end of the Mesozoic Era. So when dinosaurs roamed the Earth, there were no real grassy plains for them to stomp through. Instead there were ferns, mosses, and a knee-high layer of shrub.

EVEN OLDER THAN DINOSAURS

The Triassic Period began around 20 million years before the first dinosaurs evolved. During this time, many unusual reptiles lived on Earth. Some species didn't last very long, but others lived alongside the early dinosaurs.

Gliders

Sharovipteryx was a flying reptile that lived in Asian forests. It had very long legs and tiny arms that together supported a giant triangular flap of skin, which allowed it to glide through the air.

Fishers

Tanystropheus had an enormous neck attached to a tiny body. This puzzled paleontologists for a long time, but now they think it may have used its neck to hunt around for fish underwater while standing on the shore.

Chompers

Rhynchosaurus was a wide-bodied herbivore with a strange beak at the front of its mouth used to slice up tough plants. It was such a common animal that its fossils have been found all over the world. It lived both before and alongside the first dinosaurs.

HAPPY IN DIFFERENT HABITATS

While many species of dinosaur came and went over the millions of years that make up the Mesozoic Era, paleontologists have sorted them into three main groups.

Huge

The sauropodomorphs were the largest dinosaurs. They had long necks with small heads on the end and were plant eaters. Early sauropodomorphs, known as the "prosauropods," mostly walked on two legs, but later giants such as *Diplodocus* and *Brachiosaurus* were four-legged.

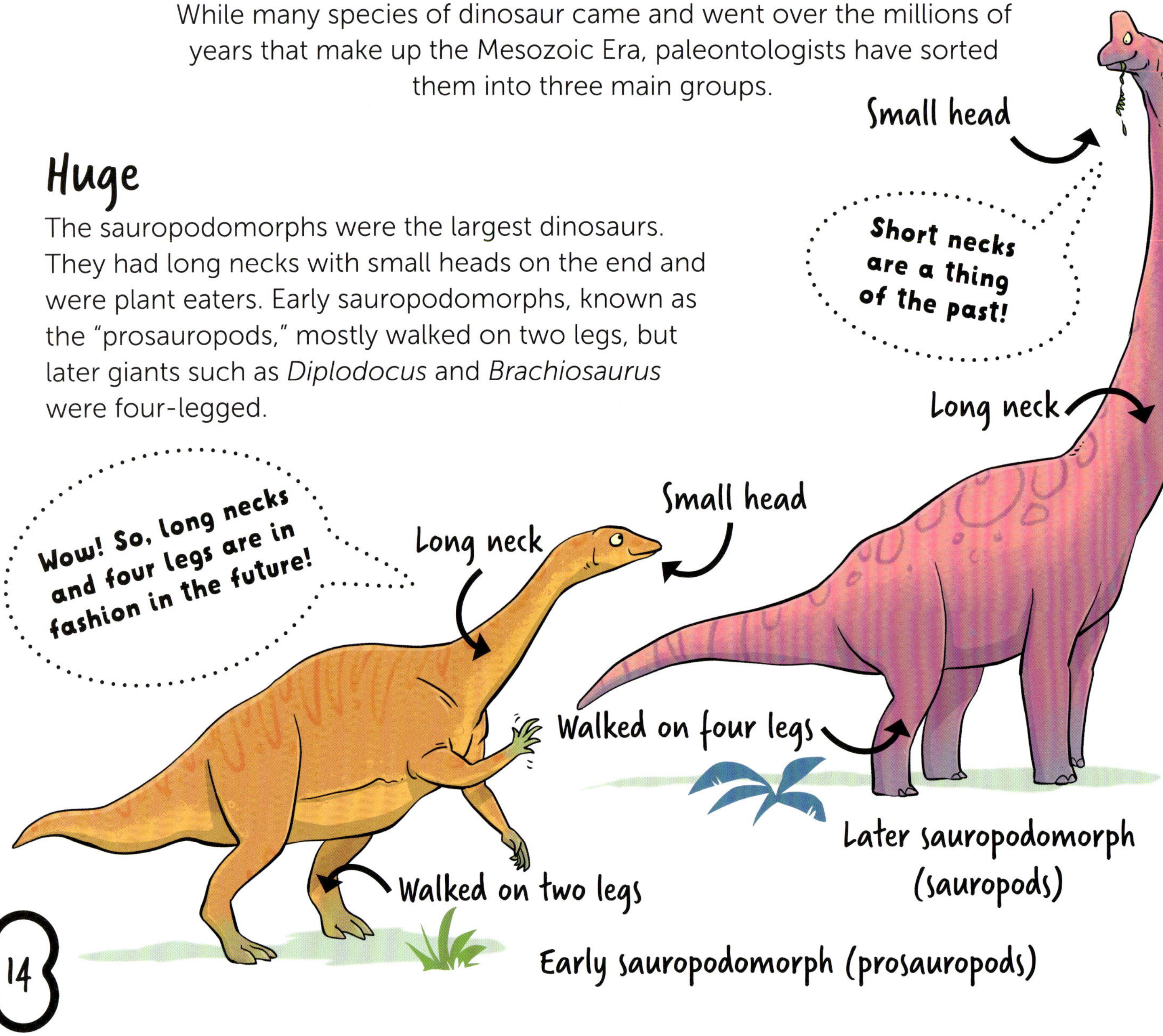

Early theropod

Toothy

The theropods were meat-eating dinosaurs, though some later moved on from meat to eat plants. All theropods walked on two legs, and while most had teeth, some switched to a beak. Later theropods had feathers, and birds evolved from them. Famous members of this group include *Tyrannosaurus*, *Allosaurus*, and *Velociraptor*.

Diverse

The ornithischians were all herbivores but were very different in size and shape. They ranged from small, two-legged animals to four-legged giants. They all had a beak at the front of their mouth and teeth at the back to help them eat plants. Famous ornithischians include the horned *Triceratops*, plated *Stegosaurus*, and the spike-thumbed *Iguanodon*.

The ornithischians

LOOK UP TO THE SKIES!

Flying reptiles, called pterosaurs, existed alongside the dinosaurs. They lived all over the world and soared over open oceans, deep in forests, and over deserts.

Flying High

Pterosaurs were the earliest vertebrates (animals with backbones) known to have evolved to fly. They didn't need to launch from trees. They could take off and fly from the ground, by flapping their wings like birds today. They had bat-like wings made of skin attached to one giant finger that they used to help them take off. Huge muscles on their arms and chests allowed them to flap their wings.

Big and Small

The smallest adult pterosaurs were about the size of a crow, and – unlike baby bats and baby birds – baby pterosaurs could also fly. The biggest pterosaurs could reach a whopping 33 feet (10 m) or more in wingspan. That's the same as a small plane!

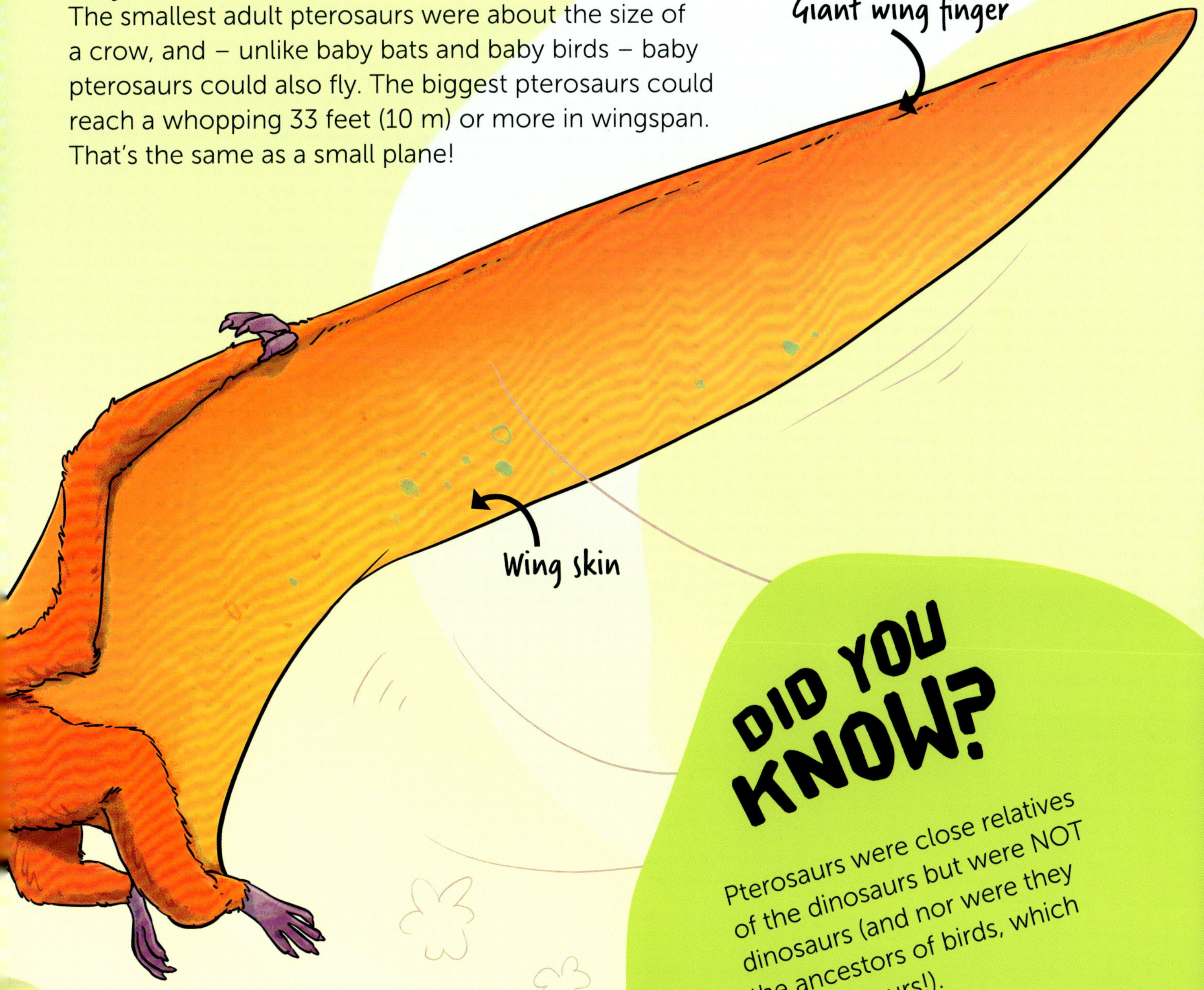

DID YOU KNOW?

Pterosaurs were close relatives of the dinosaurs but were NOT dinosaurs (and nor were they the ancestors of birds, which ARE dinosaurs!).

DOWN IN THE DEPTHS

Lots of different reptiles evolved to live in water during the Mesozoic Era. The three most famous and important species are the ichthyosaurs, plesiosaurs, and mosasaurs. Again, none of these are dinosaurs!

Big-eyed Ichthyosaurs

The ichthyosaurs were the first to appear. They had a very dolphin-like shape, were fast swimmers, and chased after fish and squid. Some grew to the size of whales and had huge eyes so they could see when diving deep into dark waters.

Long-necked Plesiosaurs

The plesiosaurs are known for their small heads, long necks, and paddle-like arms and legs. They paddled through the oceans, grabbing darting fish with their supersharp teeth.

Lengthy Mosasaurs

The mosasaurs were long-bodied animals that looked a bit like huge eels with paddles! They were mostly very large and were predators of large fish, as well as marine reptiles. If they came across a dinosaur swept out to sea, they would probably have made a meal of it too.

REPTILES

Many other types of reptile lived alongside the dinosaurs. Many were small and would have been a tasty meal for small theropods, but some of the biggest lizards could well have made a meal of a baby dinosaur.

Teeth

There used to be lots more different types of crocodile around. There were whale-like gulpers in the sea, like *Stomatosuchus* – an enormous ancient crocodile that had a long snout – and long-legged sprinters on land like *Barberenasuchus*.

Tails

Lizards and snakes were around too. Plenty of fossils have been discovered of both species, including a large snake skeleton called *Sanajeh* that was found in a dinosaur nest site. It looks like the snake was trying to eat baby sauropods from their nest!

Shells

The bony shells of terrapins and turtles preserve well, so there are lots of their fossils about. They lived in rivers, lakes, and the sea. Ground-living tortoises only evolved after the dinosaurs went extinct.

FAMILIAR FACES WITH SLIPPERY SKIN

You'd recognize lots of different animals if you went back in time to visit the dinosaurs during the Mesozoic Era. Living in water can help animals survive extinctions. This is because swimming makes it easier to move to a more suitable location as all the seas are connected. This helped some of these groups survive to the present day.

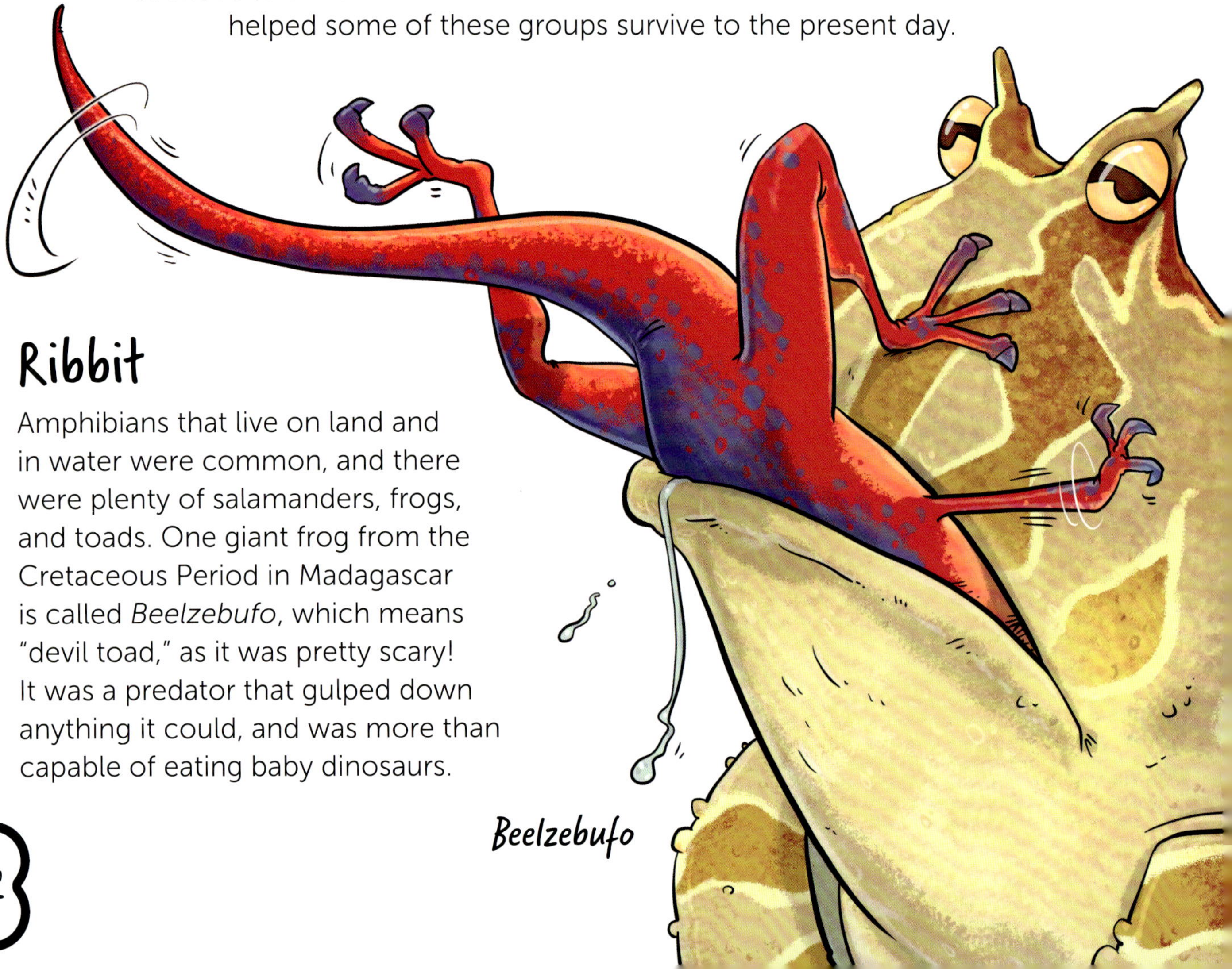

Ribbit

Amphibians that live on land and in water were common, and there were plenty of salamanders, frogs, and toads. One giant frog from the Cretaceous Period in Madagascar is called *Beelzebufo*, which means "devil toad," as it was pretty scary! It was a predator that gulped down anything it could, and was more than capable of eating baby dinosaurs.

Beelzebufo

Splash

Plenty of different kinds of shark and ray lived throughout the sea, in rivers, and in lakes. There were lots of other types of fish, too. Some were giant versions of fish we still have today, like *Arganodus* – a 7-foot (2-m) lungfish – and *Onchopristis* – a 13-foot (4-m) sawfish – both of which lived in North Africa.

FURRY FRIENDS

Early mammals lived alongside the dinosaurs and other giant reptiles. Most early mammals were small and rat-like, but scientists have found fossils of other mammals from China that look like some that are alive today.

Ancient Mammals

In trees or burrows you could find *Juramaia*, a tiny prehistoric animal from China, which looked similar to present-day shrews. These little creatures came out at night when they would be safer from predators. Soaring between the trees there lived a flying-squirrel-like glider called *Volaticotherium*, and in the lakes an otter-like swimmer named *Castorocauda*.

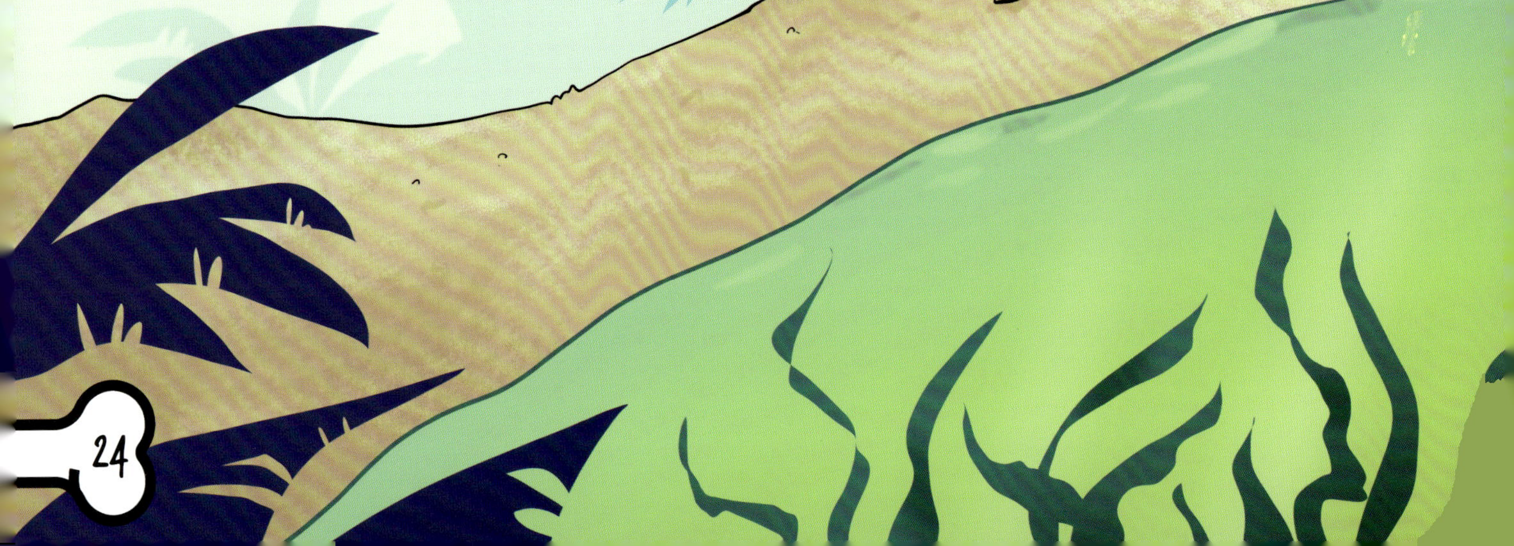

Could There Have Been Bats and Monkeys?

Although there are no fossils of them yet from the Cretaceous Period, paleontologists who have tracked the evolution of early mammals think that there may have also been some early bats and monkeys alongside the dinosaurs.

DID YOU KNOW?

There was once an early badger-like predator that was only the size of a dog, but it ate dinosaurs! It's called *Repenomamus*, and one of its fossils has the bones of a baby dinosaur inside it.

CREEPY CRAWLIES

Though the giant dinosaurs and marine reptiles tend to steal all the attention, there were lots of miniature critters during the Mesozoic Era too. Invertebrates (animals with no backbone) were present in huge numbers on land and in the water. Some of them would be familiar to you, as their descendants live on today.

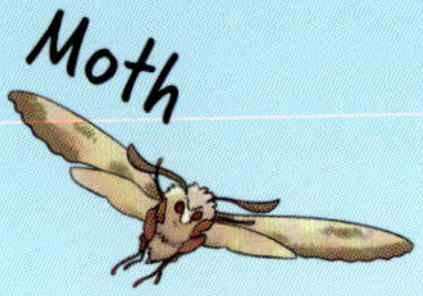

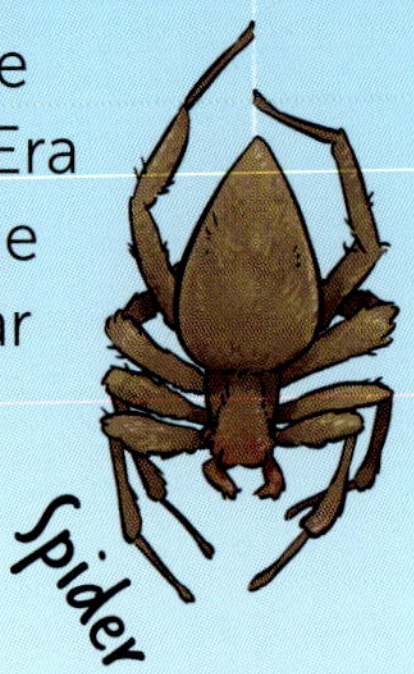

Land and Sea

On land, there were (wait for it): spiders, flies, centipedes, beetles, mayflies, ants, ticks, mosquitoes, snails, moths, and all kinds of other small invertebrates. These creatures were often a tasty meal for some dinosaurs. In the sea you could have seen clams, crabs, squid, horseshoe crabs, oysters, corals, sponges, and more.

Seashells on the Shore

Ammonites existed in huge numbers – you may have seen fossils featuring their curled shells. These were related to modern-day squid and octopus and looked similar, but lived inside a shell for protection. Many of them would have hunted other marine invertebrates or fish. They went extinct around the same time as the dinosaurs.

THE END OF THE DINOSAURS ... AND A BEGINNING

Around 65 million years ago, a large asteroid crashed into the sea near Mexico and exploded, sending huge amounts of dust into the sky.

A Dusty Explosion

The dust from the asteroid explosion blocked out the sunlight and made large parts of the world cold and dark. This caused many plants to die, as plants need sunshine to grow. This then killed off most plant-eating dinosaurs who fed on the plants. Then the many meat-eating dinosaurs who fed on the herbivores and other animals died.

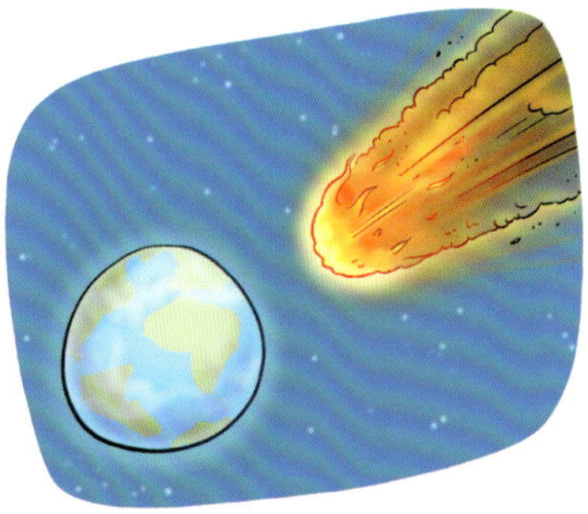

Asteroid heading toward Earth

Asteroid crashes into Earth

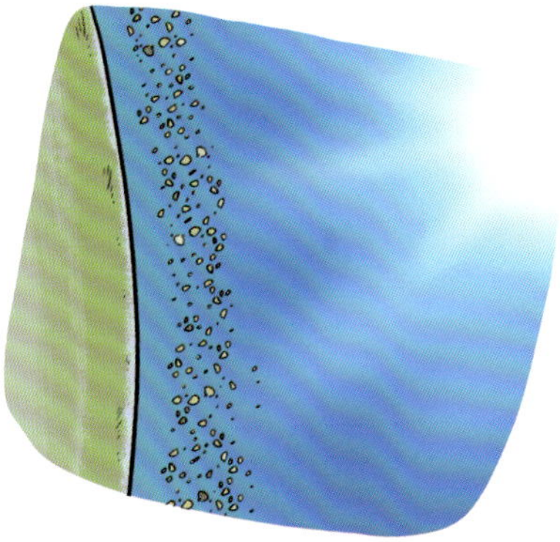

Dust from the asteroid blocks out the Sun

Lost Forever

The flying pterosaurs and marine reptiles all died out, and lots of other groups of animals and plants were lost forever, becoming extinct. Familiar groups that did survive – such as the mammals, crocodiles, and amphibians – lost lots of species.

All Change Please

The extinction gave some species new opportunities. Mammals eventually took over Earth and went on to produce and evolve into the many species that we see today (including humans!). And not all of the dinosaurs were lost: if you look around you'll see that small theropods are among us – in our parks and in our trees. That's because some birds survived the extinction and went on to produce all the species we see today.

GLOSSARY

Amphibians – a group of animals with four legs that often live on land and in water (like frogs and newts). Nearly all of them need water in order to lay their eggs there.

Descendant – an animal that lives after and is related to another animal that lived in the past.

Dinosaurs – a group of extinct reptiles that were the dominant land animals from around 230–65 million years ago. Their descendants live on today – birds.

Evolution – the natural process where, over time, species of organisms change in response to their environment.

Extinction – the complete loss of a species or group. All the members have died out.

Fossil – the remains of an ancient animal or plant (or remains from their movements, such as footprints) that have turned to stone.

Gliding – a form of flying that doesn't involve any flapping. Gliding animals lose height as they move so they need to climb to fly again.

Invertebrates – animals that do not have a backbone. This includes everything from spiders to jellyfish, to corals and snails.

Mammals – a group of animals with four legs and fur. They produce milk for their babies, which are usually born from the mother, though a few mammals lay eggs.

Marsupials – a group of mammals that carry their young in a pouch.

Ornithischians – a group of plant-eating dinosaurs. Some walked on two legs and others on four, and many of them had armor or head crests with spikes on them.

Paleontologist – a scientist who studies ancient life, which includes dinosaurs and other animals, plants, and ancient environments.

Pollen – a fine powder produced by plants that enables them to form seeds to grow new ones. It can be released in the air or carried by insects or water in order for new plants to grow elsewhere.

Pterosaurs – a group of ancient flying reptiles that lived alongside their close relatives, the dinosaurs.

Reptiles – a group of animals with four legs that usually live on land (though some live in water). They have scaly skin and either lay eggs or give birth to live young.

Sauropods – a group of large dinosaurs that had long necks and tails. They walked on four legs and ate plants.

Species – a set of animals or plants in which the members have similar features to each other and can have babies with each other.

Theropods – a group of meat-eating dinosaurs (though some switched and ate plants) that walked on two legs.

FURTHER INFORMATION

Books

Body Bits: Dead-awesome Dinosaur Body Facts by Paul Mason and Dave Smith (Wayland, 2021)

Dinosaur Infosaurus series by Katie Woolley (Wayland, 2021)

Dino-Sorted series by Sonya Newland and Izzi Howell (Gareth Stevens Publishing, 2026)

Websites

Find out about dinosaurs and prehistoric life:
kids.nationalgeographic.com/animals/prehistoric

Watch a video to learn more about the asteroid that made the dinosaurs go extinct: https://youtu.be/2B9XmiOIA4E

Explore the Natural History Museum's directory of dinosaurs:
www.nhm.ac.uk/discover/dino-directory.html

Play games, watch videos and learn about paleontology:
www.amnh.org/explore/ology/paleontology

INDEX